CREDIT CARD HACKS

What Credit Card Companies Don't Want You to Know

Copyright 2020 Ahmed Dawn

All rights reserved. No part of this book may be reproduced, in whole or in part, without the specific written permission of the author, Ahmed Dawn. The author is the sole author of the work and the sole owner of the copyright.

Disclaimer

The information in this book is for informational purposes only and no information is intended as investment, tax, accounting or legal advice, or as an offer to sell or buy or solicitation of an offer to sell or buy, or as an endorsement, recommendation or sponsorship of any product, company, security, or credit cards. The author assumes no liability for any inaccurate, delayed or incomplete information, nor for any actions taken in reliance thereon. You bear responsibility for your own financial research and decisions and should seek the advice of a qualified financial professional before making any financial decision.

CREDIT CARD HACKS

*What Credit Card Companies Don't
Want You to Know*

AHMED DAWN

Creator of Globally Popular Financial Blog
Ahmed Dawn Dot Com

Also By Ahmed Dawn

Invest Now: A Canadian's Guide to Investing

Money Hacks: How Small Changes Can Save Big Money

ABOUT THE AUTHOR

Award-winning author Ahmed Dawn is a City University of New York Economics graduate. The former Financial Advisor now works as a Data Integrity Analyst for a major Canadian wealth management corporation.

He created the globally-popular website Ahmed Dawn Dot Com (http://www.ahmeddawn.com/) and the YouTube Channel A Dawn (http://www.youtube.com/adawn) to make the world of personal finance, travel and technology easy and accessible for everyone. Invest Now is Ahmed's first book. He makes his home in the world-class city of Toronto.

This book is dedicated to all the journalists across the globe who have fallen and to those who are continuously risking their lives in the gallant fight to uphold truth and justice. Your courage and hard work are an inspiration to all of us.

If you control your credit cards, you control your future.

– Scott Bilker.

TABLE OF CONTENTS

Preface 1

Introduction 2

PART ONE 7

Chapter One: How to Use This Book 9

Chapter Two: Types of Credit Cards 11

Chapter Three: How To Pick The Right Credit Cards 13

Chapter Four: Don't Leave Home Without These Features 18

PART TWO 23

Chapter Five: How to Use Credit Card Rates 25

Chapter Six: How To Use Promotional Rate Offer 28

Chapter Seven: How to Use a Credit Card to Literally
Make Money 30

Chapter Eight: What You Need to Know About Your Credit
Score and Credit Report 32

Chapter Nine: Smarter Ways to Make Credit Card Payments 37

Chapter Ten: What Credit Card Features You Should Never Use .. 40

Chapter Eleven: Do You Really Need Credit Card Insurance? 42

Chapter Twelve: How to Use Store or Retail Credit Cards,
Including Gas and Grocery Store Cards 44

Chapter Thirteen: How to Use Prepaid Credit Cards 47

Chapter Fourteen: The Best Hidden Credit Card Perk No One
Uses: Free or Partial Free Travel 48

Chapter Fifteen: How to Travel for Free or Fly Business Class for Free or Paying Very Little 50

Chapter Sixteen: Bonus Credit Card Tips 55

Chapter Seventeen: How to Save Money on Travel or Vacation 58

Chapter Eighteen: Ahmed Dawn Dot Com & My YouTube Channel 61

Conclusion 68

PREFACE

When my parents were in their 20s, they had not seen or heard about anything like credit cards. There was some kind of concept of credit – using which consumers and merchants were able to post-dated payments for goods and services. But it was nowhere near using a piece of plastic instead of money – and such an idea back then would be preposterous.

When I was in my 20s, there were credit cards but not the widespread bizarre variety like now. Also, a credit card was not considered a necessity item, but a fancy item hovering somewhere between luxury and necessity.

These days? A credit card is no longer a luxury item, but a dire necessity. And you won't be able to walk through life from birth to death without credit cards; most hospitals and funeral homes won't serve you if you don't have a credit card in those countries where these services are not provided for free.

So instead of rejecting credit cards, embrace them. On the other hand, you have to be careful here because if you don't know the ins and outs of credit cards, credit card companies will use your ignorance to their advantage.

You should be the domain of your financial future and you should be the one to use credit cards to make and save money to your advantage. This is your future and no one else will do it for you. The credit card techniques you learn and apply today will have an enormous impact in the future. Don't wait. This is the time. Let's begin.

INTRODUCTION

Why This Book?

With the rapid evolution of technology throughout the passage of time, we are witnessing a vast change in every aspect of life. We can buy plane tickets at home and transact business with someone in a place far beyond our borders.

Not all the products and services technology is bringing will remain the same in the future. Some will stay, some will become obsolete. However, these changes will not go away and will only become better as superior products and services to replace them. A credit card is such a product.

I cannot guarantee you that after 20 or 30 years credit cards will look and feel the same way they do today. But I will tell you this: credit cards are here to stay and although they may change in the future, it will only be for the better. And that's why Credit Cards Hacks is here to show you how to make full use of this great tool (your credit card) to make your life better and richer.

Don't Listen to Them – They Are Being Unrealistic

If people such as financial professionals or friends tell you to avoid credit cards because they are evil, don't listen to them because they are being unrealistic. Living in this modern age, it is not possible to live your life to the fullest without credit cards. Embrace it, instead of denying it.

Stop Right Now and Don't Buy Credit Card Hacks

This book will not do any good if you just read it and put it away once you are done with it, without applying anything mentioned herein. If your intention is not to use the procedures described here and just to buy this book for the sake of buying, I ask you to stop right now, do not buy this book, and save yourself some money.

Credit Card Hacks Is Not A Get-Rich Scam or A Promise to Make You A Millionaire

Yes, this book will show you how to make and save money with credit cards. However, if you are expecting to be an instant millionaire, this is not the right book for you. I ask you to move on and try something else.

Credit Card Hacks Is Not A Book About Credit Card Debt

If you are looking for a book to manage your credit card debts, this is not the book for you. The techniques mentioned in this book will work the best when you pay your balances in full every month.

Frequently Asked Questions

If you have read my first book Invest Now, you already know that I like to do things differently. Introductions do not usually feature a FAQ section, but I started adding a FAQ section in Invest Now and will continue to do so for other books. So here I will answer some basic questions you may have about me and this book through these frequently asked questions.

Who are you?

I am the author of the award-winning book Invest Now and most recently published Money Hacks. Also, I am the author of the popular personal finance website http://www.ahmeddawn.com/ that attracts thousands of visitors across the globe daily.

Why is this book so thin?

Have you heard of information overload? In this digital age, we are always bombarded with information and our brain capacity allows us to grasp and use only so much. If you read a 400-page book with thousands of tips, what will you most likely do at the end? You will just put it on your shelf to collect dust or it will be lost somewhere on your smartphone or computer. I have eliminated chitchat, small talk and stories of John and Jane, and stocked the book with only the stuff you need to know.

How much money will I save?

This is a hard question to answer, honestly. How much money you will save mainly depends on your lifestyle and spending habits. Each chapter will represent a different opportunity for different individuals. However, I will tell you this with confidence: only applying the bonus chapter can save you something that you would never thought possible.

OK, I like your writing style explaining simply how to apply credit card techniques. How can I get more of your articles or follow up with you beyond this book?

I am the author of the popular financial website Ahmed Dawn Dot Com at http://www.ahmeddawn.com/ which attracts thousands of readers daily across the globe. I suggest you visit my site on a regular basis for more articles on personal finance. Also, I have a popular YouTube Channel at http://www.youtube.com/adawn offering nearly 700 videos on a variety of topics, including credit cards and travel.

Part One

CHAPTER ONE

How to Use This Book

Credit Card Hacks Is Designed for Global Readers

Before we begin, I would like to clarify that this book is written for no single country, but for all countries across the globe. Whether you are reading this book in Manila or Manitoba, the techniques can be applied, as long as you can get the basics.

Having said that, I understand that all the techniques mentioned here may not work 100 percent in your country. But there is no way you won't be able to apply at least some of the techniques in your country to save and make money.

Examples Are Kept Minimal

One of the challenges in writing a book for global readers is to come up with real examples that are applicable in every country. For that reason, I tried to avoid giving examples of real credit card names or companies. If examples are used, they are in simple and understandable terms.

Internet Search Keywords

As you go through Credit Card Hacks, you will come across mentions of Internet search keywords or phrases. These examples are to help you find appropriate credit cards for those techniques mentioned in that chapter by searching online in your country.

No Definition Required

I have skipped writing about the definition of a credit card or how it works, as this is redundant and unnecessary. If you are reading this book, you already know what a credit card is – and my objective is to deliver only what you need to know...keeping this book as simple and precise as possible.

CHAPTER TWO

Types of Credit Cards

Is It That Simple?

There are hundreds of types of credit cards, but they can be very easily boiled down into two types: those that come with rewards and those that do not.

Credit Cards without Rewards

Whether you call it a basic or standard credit card, this type is the original version of credit cards and still exists everywhere. Basic credit cards are still used by lots of people and can be used for transactions just like regular credit cards.

If you are reading this book and still use basic credit cards, I would ask you to get rid of them once you finish this book and decide on a reward credit card. You will not be able to make any money using a basic credit card.

Credit Cards with Rewards

Let's go over some credit card names:
- Cash Back Credit Cards
- Reward Points Credit Cards
- Travel Points Credit Cards
- Hotel Points Credit Cards

- Airline Points Credit Cards
- Gas Points Credit Cards
- Retail Store Credit Cards
- Coffee Shop Credit Cards

Do all these names look different to you? Although the names are different, the one thing they all have in common is that they are all rewards credit cards. These days, you will find rewards cards from all sorts of businesses and services and it can be confusing to get a suitable card that meets your needs and allows you to make money. That's why in the next chapter I will go over some must-have information you should look at when picking your rewards credit cards.

CHAPTER THREE

How To Pick The Right Credit Cards

In this chapter, I will cover the different types of reward cards and how you can make a decision on what types of rewards cards you should be getting.

This Chapter Is All You Need

Let's say you spent a few dollars buying this book and don't want to read the whole book. If you only read this chapter and use your knowledge to pick the best rewards cards, your investment of buying this book will pay off. I will go through some materials you need to know to get credit cards that will make you money. However, keep in mind that I will not be able to recommend specific cards, as I could not possibly imagine which country you are reading this book from. You will have to do further research using what you just learned to find the best cards in your country.

All Reward Cards Are Not Created Equally

It is important to understand that not all reward cards are the same. Two cash back rewards cards or travel rewards cards from two different banks can look the same with similar names, but when it comes to giving you rewards the differences can be night and day.

I will go over some of the basics of different types of rewards cards so you have a clear understanding of what they are.

Cash Back Rewards Cards

These are the most basic, popular reward cards. You can't go wrong keeping a cash back reward card when you don't want to travel, buy merchandise, or simply are not sure about other reward cards.

Various cards offer percentages of cash back ranging from very low (.05 percent) to very high (3 percent). Pay attention to these percentages, as credit card companies try to trick consumers with higher returns that may not be easy to achieve. For example, there can be various levels of rewards for various types of purchases. They will tell you it's 3 percent cash back, but that 3 percent cash back can only apply to limited types of purchases or for a limited time only, such as select grocery stores or only for the first 4 months – and everything else is 1 percent.

If a cash back credit card has an annual fee you need to be even more cautious. On paper, these cards might offer a higher cash back return than no-fee cash back cards. What they are not telling you is that to earn that higher return you will have to spend very high amounts on your card annually to cover the annual fee, and then you can make money after that. However, you might be able to make more money with an annual fee card that pays a higher return if you spend a lot of money.

Another catch to be aware of is that cash rewards earnings can be tiered. For example, you make 0.50 percent on the first $5,000 you spend and then earn 1 percent on the next $5,000, and so on.

If you carry a balance, you will not be able to make money because you are paying 20 to 25 percent interest on your balance.

To find the most suitable cash back credit card in your country, research online to compare various cards and then decide on the best one according to your needs. There are many comparison websites offering various tools that will show the details such as annual fees, percentages of returns, if there are any caps, how much you need to spend to cover the annual fee, etc. Do not rush to pick a credit card without researching thoroughly. Use these Internet keywords to search:

- compare cash back credit cards
- top cash back credit cards
- best cash rewards credit cards, etc.

Travel Rewards Cards

Whether you call them frequent flyer miles rewards cards, airline miles rewards cards, Aero Plan Rewards cards, Air Miles Rewards Cards, or something else, these are all travel rewards cards and they work in similar ways.

Travel Rewards cards are very popular rewards cards, like cash rewards cards. However, one point to consider when choosing travel rewards cards is that if you don't travel it may not make sense to keep them because if you redeem your points for something else other than travel you will get much less value.

When picking a travel rewards card, make sure you get the best value in cents and in case of an annual fee card make sure your fees are justified; meaning your annual fee cost exceeds the rewards and benefits you get.

Here is one simple example to show you why you need to keep an eye on annual fees. Let's say your ABC Travel Rewards Card has an annual fee of $100 and rewards you 1 point for each dollar you spend. If one point is worth 1 cent, you will have to spend $10,000 a year just to cover its annual fee.

Some travel rewards cards restrict redeeming points by imposing blackout periods, seat restrictions, booking fees, minimum points requirement, etc. Some cards' points even have expiration dates and become worthless if you don't use them in time. Keep these things in mind when researching travel rewards cards.

Just like cash back credit cards, if you carry a balance on your credit cards and expect to make money, it will not work. Another thing to keep an eye on is a sign-up bonus. I will talk about this in detail in another chapter on how you can master travel rewards cards' sign-up bonus offer to travel free and make money.

To find the best rewards card for you, use the Internet to research thoroughly and take your time to make your decision. Some search keywords you can use include:

- Travel rewards cards
- Travel rewards cards comparison
- Best travel rewards cards

Other Rewards Cards

There are so many other bizarre rewards cards that I could easily write another book on them. Here are just a few:

- General points rewards cards
- Gas rewards cards
- Hotel rewards cards
- Airline rewards cards
- Coffee shop rewards cards
- Retail rewards cards

You get the idea. I won't be surprised if I see a rewards card from the corner convenience store.

The rewards card you choose should be the one that gives you maximum rewards. Try to stick with travel rewards cards and cash back rewards cards, as these two in general offer the most value. However, depending on where you are, if you find any other types of cards giving you more returns, go ahead and use those cards.

In the next chapter, I will discuss some features you need to know and look for in your rewards cards.

A Full Chapter on How to Travel Free and Make Money

Just a heads up: There will be a full chapter in the end where I will show you how you can travel for free and make money using your travel rewards cards every year, year after year.

CHAPTER FOUR

Don't Leave Home Without These Features

Competition Benefits Everyone

There are so many credit card companies competing against each other to get your business that they have no choice but to throw as many features and benefits as possible at you to stay in business. You can benefit from these features by making sure your credit cards have as many as possible. You also need to know what these features really mean and how to utilize them. I will go over some common features and benefits you need to make sure your credit cards offer.

Price Protection

If you buy something and find it at a lower price within a certain amount of days (the amount varies depending on the card), your card company will refund the difference.

Purchase Security

In case of a lost, stolen, or damaged item within a certain number of days, your credit card company will replace/reimburse/repair it.

Extended Warranty/Return Policy

Your credit card company will double the manufacturer's warranty and will extend return days from 30 to 60 or 90 days. If the retailer does not accept the return, your credit card company will refund you up to a certain amount.

Auto Rental Collision/Loss Damage Coverage

If you decline a rental company's insurance and waive their collision damage waiver, your credit card company will cover you for these insurances when you charge the full cost of your car rental to your credit card.

Chargeback

If retailers provide you unsatisfactory goods or services and refuse to refund your money, your credit card company will refund you and charge the item back to the retailer.

Zero Liability

In case of fraudulent and unauthorized use of your credit card, you are protected and pay nothing.

Delayed/Lost Baggage Insurance

If your checked baggage is lost or delayed for more than a certain amount of hours, your credit card company will reimburse you to replace essential items up to a certain amount.

Trip Cancellation and Interruption Insurance

If covered causes prevent you from starting or completing your trip, your credit card will cover you for eligible expenses up to a certain amount.

Emergency Travel Assistance

In case of an emergency when you are travelling, your credit card company will provide various services such as medical consultation, lost luggage assistance, legal and bail bond assistance, emergency cash, emergency transportation, emergency ticket replacement and travel documents replacement, and much more.

Travel Medical Insurance

This feature is like buying travel insurance and not paying anything because it is already included in your credit card. This feature could save you $300-$400 per trip.

Free Concierge Services

Concierge service is like having your own personal assistant and they will do many things you request for free. I will elaborate on this in a moment.

There Is More to It Than Meets The Eye

Whenever you are choosing a credit card, whether it's a cash or travel rewards card, try to pick the card which gives you the most rewards and some of the features I mentioned in this chapter. In your country, you may not get some of the features I mentioned or may get more than what I mentioned here. The point is that you should spend some time researching to get a credit card with the most rewards and features in your country.

However, sometimes you may not be able to exceed the cost of the annual fee of a premium card in terms of the value worth rewards points, but you will exceed its annual fee worth if you factor in the services and benefits you enjoy.

Here is an example to elaborate. Let's say you have a travel rewards card that offers most of the features I mentioned for an annual fee of $120. To recover this $120 annual fee, you would have to spend at least $700 a month, and there is no way you will spend that much on your credit card. So the question is, is it still possible to receive more value (than your annual fee) without spending $700 on this card?

You are probably thinking the answer is no, but surprisingly enough the answer is yes. Let me show you how. Let's say you make one trip per year and you don't pay travel insurance. You get $300 (possibly more) right there, plus it makes you an additional $180 after paying the annual fee. Next, let's say you use its concierge service to let them do some research for you, including making reservations at restaurants, buying movie tickets, and so on. The value for all these services is priceless because they are saving you so much time, money, and hassle.

Before I end this chapter, let me give you just a few examples of what my credit card concierge service did for me in the past:

- Booked a hotel
- Made a restaurant reservation
- Bought a Greyhound bus ticket and mailed it to my address
- Bought a movie ticket and mailed it to my address

- Prepared a report suggesting how to go to Pennsylvania, where to stay, where to shop, etc.
- Prepared a report suggesting various resorts and flight options on my Dominican trip

Part Two

CHAPTER FIVE

How to Use Credit Card Rates

If You Don't Carry A Balance

If you pay your balance in full each month, credit card rates should not be a matter you need to worry about. I encourage you to not carry a balance to take full advantage of what credit cards have to offer. However, I will still touch base on credit card rates a little bit as it's good to know how it works and it will help those who carry balances.

APR

APR or Annual Percentage Rate is used to describe credit card interest rates. A single credit card can have various different APRs for different transactions. For example, regular transactions, cash advances, balance transfers can each have a different APR.

Variable Rate or Non-Variable Rate

A variable rate is determined by adding a set of numbers to a reference rate. This reference rate has different names in different countries such as prime rate, overnight rate, fed rate, short-term lending rate, and so on. These numbers are nothing but a number or rate determined by the central bank, and the financial institutions charge each other to borrow/lend money for overnight or short term.

A non-variable rate is not tied to a prime rate but set by your credit card company. Credit card companies can change rates from variable to non-variable or vice versa anytime.

How Credit Cards Calculate Interest

Please see the example article mentioned in the chapter Ahmed Dawn Dot Com. The methods mentioned in this article are used in most countries.

How to Get the Best Interest Rates on Credit Cards

If you carry balances on your credit cards, follow these tips and start working right away to find better rates for you. The amounts you can save on interest can be staggering. For example, if you can only cut down, let's say, 3 percent interest on 20 percent, making the interest you pay 17 percent. There are online calculators you can use to see how much money you will actually save. Just search for "credit card calculators" online.

Decide upon 5 to 10 credit card companies in your country and visit their websites or call them to find out what kinds of rates they can offer if you transfer your balances. Walk to your local bank branch and ask if they can offer you better rates if you transfer your balances.

It's good to get promotional lower interest rates, but also concentrate on what rates you are paying in an ongoing basis.

Another way to reduce your interest rate is by simply asking for it. Call your current credit card customer service line and negotiate a better rate. Be polite and confident on the phone and tell them that you are calling to find out if they can offer better rates to match other rates you have received from competitors. The reason you are calling them is because you wanted to check with them first before switching to other companies, as you like their services and want to stay with them. If you hear "No", ask for a manager or supervisor and try it again.

The above procedures have always worked for many people to lower interest rates, and you should be able to lower yours as well. The reason credit card companies don't want to lose you that easily is because in general credit card companies spend around $500 - $1000 to acquire a client and it's in their best interest to keep you as many years as they can.

CHAPTER SIX

How To Use Promotional Rate Offer

In this chapter, I will cover related topics such as how to identify a low rate offer and what else to look for. Let's begin with not only for new cards.

Not Only for New Cards

When you apply for new cards, you may get a special lower rate offer for a certain amount of months. However, from time to time, credit card companies will offer you special low rates for a certain amount of time and you should take full advantage of this to borrow money for cheap.

How to Identify a Low Rate Offer

Special low rate offers can come in your regular mail, via email, or on credit card companies' websites or smartphone apps when you log in. These can even show on the main page before you log in. Also, you can call your card companies and ask them if they have any special rate promotions going on or if they can offer you any special rates.

Carefully Go Over Terms and Conditions

If you received blank cheques (checks) in the mail, make sure they are not for regular cash advances and for special lower rates. Check how long the rate will last, if there is a balance transfer fee or admin fee when it expires, and so on. If you are using a card to take advantage of a lower rate, do not use that card for anything else because if you keep using that card for other purchases you will pay a higher interest rate on your new transactions. The reason is because credit card companies apply your payments towards your old transactions first and new transactions will incur higher charges, as you took advantage of special promotional rates and not paying your balance in full until the promotion ends.

If you are charged a onetime balance transfer fee of 1 percent to get a 3 percent special rate offer, it's still a good deal because your total rate still stays way below a lot of other credit card's rates.

Another thing you need to be very careful about when using a special rate offer is its expiration date. Make a note of the expiration date on your smartphone or online calendar and set a reminder about 7 to 10 days ahead. This is when you will pay off your loan, as you don't want to be delayed even a single day paying off your special rate loan. It is possible that some cards might charge you full regular interest rate for the full term on the special rate offer loan if you miss a single payment or are a single day late paying it off. You don't want that to happen.

CHAPTER SEVEN

How to Use a Credit Card to Literally Make Money

In this chapter, I will discuss the possibilities of making money using promotional rate offers.

Don't Let Go of Promotional Rate Offers

In the previous chapter, I talked about promotional rate offers from your credit card companies for both new and old credit cards. If you know how to use these offers, this one feature of credit cards can make you money for real. I will discuss some of the methods you can use towards increasing your net worth.

Option 1 – Pay Off Other High Interest Debts

Use your promotional credit card rate offers to pay off all other high-interest debts, such as other credit cards, car loans, retail store credit cards, or anything else you can think of that is charging you more than your promotional rates. How much money you can save? It all depends on what kinds of offers you have.

Let's look at one example. Let's say you have a $5000 loan on your credit card that charges 20 percent annual interest. Your interest cost per month is about $83.33. Now, if you have a 3 percent promotional rate offer for one year, your monthly interest cost is $12.50. How much money you are making monthly? $83.33 - $12.50 = $70.83. Not bad, right? Making money or saving money this way is not difficult and very safe. Anyone should be able to do it without hesitation.

Option 2 – Buy Investments

Let me start with a word of caution. This procedure requires in-depth financial knowledge of the stock markets and there are risks involved. You should not try this unless you are knowledgeable enough to deal with financial investments and have traded financial products such as stocks, funds, ETFs, etc. in the past. Always consult a qualified financial professional before making any investment decision. No investments are guaranteed and you may lose some or all of your money.

How you do it? Let's say you have a promotional 3 percent offer available on $5,000.00 for one year. You know ETFs or dividend-paying stocks that pay a 5 percent dividend and have growth opportunities. So your spread will be on your interest of 2 percent plus possible growth from capital appreciation (increase in value). So in this scenario, you are making $8.30 per month from the interest spread and you will make even more money if your investments go up. For example, you are selling your $5,000 investments once the promotional rate offer is about to expire at $6,000. So you will make another $1,000 from the capital gain.

The above scenario is possible, but it will only work if your investments meet your expectation to go higher in value. The reverse can happen as well. If your investments go down in value, you will lose money. And in the world of investments, anything is possible. You can lose some or all your money. That's why option 2 is not for everyone. If you are financially knowledgeable and can take risks, consult a financial professional to check if option 2 is for you.

CHAPTER EIGHT

What You Need to Know About Your Credit Score and Credit Report

You have come across these terms so many times in the news and other places. Now let's get a good grasp of what they really mean.

What Is A Credit Report?

A credit report is an "overview" of your credit history. A credit report can show information on you (name, DOB, address, work), your paying habits, what debts you have, your public records (tax liens, court judgements, etc.), and a list of those who requested your credit report. Keep in mind that based on your country, some information may or may not appear on your report.

What information does not appear on your report? This can vary from country to country, but in general, any bankruptcy that was discharged seven years ago, any convictions, judgements, tax liens after seven years, and criminal charges that were dropped or pardoned are not on your credit report.

Why Your Credit Report is Important

Lenders, employers, insurance companies, landlords, utility companies, and many other institutions review your credit report and make decisions on whether to offer you their services or not.

Where Is This Credit Report Coming From?

Depending on where you live, there are reporting agencies on credit bureaus that collect, maintain, and provide this information to others in the form of a credit report.

What Kind of Rights You Have

To protect consumers, each country has some sort of consumer protection act or law. These acts or laws are in general the following:

- Reporting agencies must be registered with the government.
- What can appear on the report.
- Who can request the report.
- Consumers' right to know who is requesting their reports.
- Right to correct inaccurate information.

Can Anyone Request Your Report?

By law, any organizations requesting your report must have your consent.

What Can You Do If You're Denied Something Because of Your Credit Report?

If you are denied something such as a credit card, credit increase request, or employment, you have the right to receive a free credit report within ten days.

Also, organizations may need to reveal what information they used to deny you.

No One Can Erase or Fix Your Bad Credit

Beware of those misleading ads claiming they can fix your credit report or erase your bad credit for fees. The facts that affect your credit score cannot be erased by someone and these facts will follow their course to stay on your report until they complete their time cycle. Only you can improve your credit report by acting responsibly and taking the proper steps in the right direction.

How to Correct Errors on Your Credit Report

If you find errors on your credit report, you can ask reporting agencies to fix it. You may be able to call them or write them to fix these errors. Check the credit bureau website in your country to find out how to request to fix errors.

Once errors are fixed, reporting agencies may need to notify those who requested your credit report in the last 60 days.

What Is A Credit Score?

A credit score is a score of your overall financial health. Lenders and other institutions use this score to figure out how good or bad you are as a customer to lend money with what kind of risks.

In North America, usually a credit score runs from 300 to 900. The higher your score is, the better customer you are, as you pose a lower risk for the lender and will get better deals from lenders with lower interest rates.

What Determines Your Credit Score?

There are five main factors that determine your score.

1. Payment History (35%) – This is the biggest factor. It's based on anything related to how you paid cards or loans, such as if you paid on time, had any late payments, bankruptcy or judgements, past-due accounts, etc.
2. Amounts Owed (30%) – This is based on your all balances, what proportion of available credit you are using, how many accounts you are using, etc.
3. Length of Credit History (15%) – How long your accounts have been active. The longer the better.
4. New Credit (10%) – This includes how many times a credit check has been done in the past, how many new accounts you opened, and how much of an interval there is in between opening accounts. Doing all these frequently hurt your credit score.
5. Types of Credit Used (10%) – Having a variety of credit accounts such as credit cards, mortgages, investment loans, etc. is good for your credit score.

The above breakdown is common and widely accepted in North America. It can be slightly different in your country. Check the credit bureau website in your country to find out what the exact breakdown is.

Why It Is Important to Have a Higher Credit Score

It's simple – the higher your credit score is, the lower you pay in interest, and the more money you save. If you can keep your score on the higher level, you will get better deals from lenders and then you can turn loans at very low rates to purchase investments or properties to make money. This is how rich people make money (leverage) without using their own money.

How to Improve and Maintain a Good Credit Score

Maintaining a higher score is not as difficult as it may look. You need to follow some simple rules such as:

- Paying bills on time.
- Paying balances in full (if you can't pay in full, pay at least the minimum or more than the minimum).
- Not going over the credit limit.
- Not applying too frequently for credit.
- Paying off debts quickly.
- Going through your credit report once every 2 years (or every year) and correcting any errors.

How to Know Your Credit Score and Credit Report

You can obtain your credit report for free, but you may need to pay to get your credit score. This varies from country to country. For example, in the USA and Canada, you can obtain your credit score for free.

However, you may also be able to obtain your credit score for free when you are applying for car loans, mortgages, credit cards, etc. I have had mixed success in obtaining my credit score for free in Canada. I asked banks to disclose my credit score when I applied for credit and I never had success, but I always had success from my mortgage broker/institution when I asked.

CHAPTER NINE

Smarter Ways to Make Credit Card Payments

In this chapter, I will talk about how paying your credit card bills a little differently can save you money and can save you from missing paying your minimum payments.

Make Early Payments

Most credit card companies use the average daily balance method to calculate interest. If you are making one or several small payments before your due date, your average daily balance will be lower, and you will save money on interest. So pay as early as possible and as often as possible. This method saves you money if you carry balances. If you pay your balance in full, it really does not matter how often or early you pay as long as you are paying in full before the due date.

Do Not Miss Your Due Date

If you are paying your balances in full each time, missing your due date or making a late payment can make you pay interest on your entire balance for that month. It may not be a big deal to pay interest only one month, but it risks the possibility of impacting your credit score because some credit card companies will report if you are only one payment late.

If you carry balances or use promotional rates, missing a payment can hit you hard. Financial institutions will increase your rate to a much higher percentage or wipe out your promotional rate and put you back on their regular rate if you miss a payment. To avoid all this, make your payment long before your due date.

Understand and Utilize Your Interest-Free Grace Period

A grace period is the amount of time you have to pay off your credit card balances without paying interest after your billing cycle ends. Credit card companies usually offer 21 to 25-day grace periods these days, but most companies are shrinking it to 21 days. I have seen in the past some cards gave 28 to 31-day grace periods and still there might be some credit cards that offer longer periods.

What does this grace period mean to you? It's an opportunity to use credit card companies' money for free for a few days. Think of it this way: your credit card companies are giving you money for free and they are paying 20% interest for you while you use their money and pay it back before the due date. Call your credit card companies or check their websites to see how long their grace periods are. The more days, the better. Also, keep in mind that there are no grace periods for cash advances or balance transfers because interest kicks in right away the moment you use them.

Here is an example of a grace period:

- Your credit card billing cycle is Jan 1 – Jan 31.
- Your credit card offers a 21-day grace period.
- Your payment due date is Feb 20.
- If you make a purchase on Jan 2, you will have 21 days in your grace period from Jan 31 (the last day of your billing cycle) as long as you pay your balance in full by the current month's due date (Feb 20).

As you can see from the above example, by understanding these dates (your billing cycle, grace period, and due date), you can actually have more days of free money from credit card companies when you pay off your balances. For example, if you make purchases in the days close to when the billing cycle starts, you will have more days. If you purchase near the end cycle date, you will have fewer days.

CHAPTER TEN

What Credit Card Features You Should Never Use

Credit Card Hacks is about all the features and benefits credit cards offer and making the best use of them to get the most out of your credit cards. However, there is one particular feature you must avoid at any cost so credit card companies can't rip you off.

Say No to Cash Advances

A cash advance is a feature that allows you to take out cash from your credit cards. There are several ways you can do it and credit card companies make it easy to take out cash so you can have easy access to a cash advance. For example, you can call them to put money into your bank account, you can walk into a branch to walk out with cash, or you can use cheques (checks) they are sending you in the mail often.

A Cash Advance Cuts Three Ways

The problem with a cash advance is that it makes you lose money in 3 ways from the moment you do it.

1. The first fee you will pay when you use a cash advance is a transaction fee. It varies, but usually credit card companies charge 1 to 5 percent fees.
2. You start paying skyrocketing interest the moment you get a cash advance. This interest rate can be 25 to 40 percent. Yes, a

cash advance generates more interest charges than regular purchases.

3. To make you lose more money, credit card companies will not consider that you paid off your balances if you do not pay off all your balances in full. What this means is that as long as you are not making your balance zero, you will continue to pay high interest charges on balances, even if you had paid off the exact cash advance you took but did not make your balance zero.

After all this, do you really want to use this feature and have your credit card companies have a skyrocketing interest party on you?

The worst example of using a cash advance I can think of is taking out cash at casinos, losing all that money, and keep paying 40 percent on that month after month. Is this plain stupid, moronic, or deplorable?

So yes; say NO to cash advances.

CHAPTER ELEVEN

Do You Really Need Credit Card Insurance?

Credit card insurance is a feature that pays off your monthly payments if you lose your job or become sick. It is supposed to pay off your balances in case of death as well. So the question is, do you need this insurance or not?

Not So Easily

Credit card companies will try to sell you this insurance by convincing you of the many benefits credit card insurance offers. This is because they make a lot of money if they can hook you with this. The cost can be 1 to 3 percent, or even more, of your outstanding balance.

However, what they will not tell you is that there are many strings attached to this insurance when you need to utilize it. For example, you may not be covered for any pre-existing health conditions or if you lose your job because of your own fault, and so on. Even worse, if you do qualify, the minimum payments may last only for a limited time, such as a year.

Beware of The Tricks Card Companies Use

Card companies play nasty tricks to make you buy this insurance. Some of the tricks are:

- Not explaining that buying this insurance is optional.

- Attaching it to your credit card account without your knowledge or full disclosure.
- Telemarketers sign you up, saying it's free and then keep charging after the free trial period.
- Not telling you it won't cover pre-existing or some other conditions.
- Not telling you it may not cover your job loss if you are at fault.
- Not telling you that the insurance will only pay monthly minimums for a limited time.

Do You Need This Insurance?

To make your credit cards work for you and make you money, I recommend you pay off your balances in full every month. For that reason, you will not need any credit card insurance.

However, those who cannot live without carrying balances and insist on having insurance for peace of mind, you can shop for a life and disability insurance policy which will likely cover your credit cards in case anything happens. If you already have life and disability insurance, you may already be protected. Find out more by checking what your insurance covers.

CHAPTER TWELVE

How to Use Store or Retail Credit Cards, Including Gas and Grocery Store Cards

Store credit cards have both advantages and disadvantages. I will touch base on both, so you know what to use and what to avoid. And yes, if you use them cautiously you can make money as well.

What Are Store Credit Cards?

These are credit cards offered by retailers or stores, such as The Gap, Wal-Mart, Best Buy, Loblaw's, etc. to encourage consumers to spend more money by offering perks and rewards. These cards are usually co-branded with Visa or MasterCard.

What to Avoid

As store credit cards charge very high interest, usually 30% or more, avoid these cards at any cost if you don't intend to pay your balances in full.

However, you can take advantage of their promotional offers and this is the only time when you don't have to pay your balances in full – which I will discuss shortly.

How to Use Store Credit Cards

Let's look at when or how to use store credit cards.

To Establish New Credit: If you do not have any credit cards yet, applying for a store credit card to get started is not a bad idea because approval requirements are more relaxed than a regular credit card and you can start building your credit history.

Instant Discount: If you are making a large purchase, you can apply for a store credit card and get 10 to 15 percent off right on the spot. However, be careful if you are going to apply for a loan or mortgage in the near future, as it will lower your credit score.

Promotional Financing: Most retailers offer "buy now, pay later" options with their credit cards. Sometimes these offers can last 2 to 3 years with no payments and no interest. Some stores will require you to pay only minimum payments (no interest charged) and some stores may not need you to pay any monthly minimum payments. You may need to pay a onetime admin fee for them, but they are still good deals to save money.

Be cautious if you are using this extended financing offer. If you fail to pay your due amount by even $1 less or 1 day late, you will be charged full interest at a high rate for the entire length of your promotion.

Other Perks: Store credit cards might offer various benefits not available for everyone. For example, you may receive an extended return policy, extended insurance, free shipping, free gift wrapping, and so on. Some retailers even have rewards programs based on how much you spend.

Gas Credit Card: Gas credit cards are co-branded credit cards offered by gas station retailers. Depending on the type of card, you may be able to use it at all gas stations or specific gas stations to make money.

The way these credit cards are structured is that you earn rewards points or get discounts per litre of gas you buy. You can increase your savings if you use your gas cards to make everyday purchases.

Gas credit cards can save you in fuel cost by 5 to 6 percent or can save on cost per litre by 7 to 10 cents. However, the features and benefits offered by gas credit cards are limited and not as rich as other credit cards.

Grocery Credit Cards: These work the same way as gas credit cards, but you receive grocery points to buy groceries instead of gasoline.

When I had a grocery credit card in the past, I was able to accumulate $200 - $300 every 2 years or so.

The problems with grocery credit cards are that they will not offer various features like travel rewards or cash rewards cards. But depending on your lifestyle, if you think you can make money with grocery cards more than other rewards cards, you should stick to grocery credit cards.

CHAPTER THIRTEEN
How to Use Prepaid Credit Cards

Prepaid credit cards are sort of a hybrid of gift card and credit card. You can use these just like regular credit cards, but there are some limitations.

Features Prepaid Cards Offer

You can buy some prepaid cards only one time and some can be reloaded later on. There can be an annual fee or a usage fee (one time or each time you use) associated with prepaid cards. There could be other fees as well, so make sure you read all the fine prints before you buy.

When to Use Prepaid Cards

Prepaid cards can be used as gift cards or to give your kids so you don't need to worry about them going over the limit. If you are concerned about security when you travel or shop online, these cards can also come in handy.

When Not to Use Prepaid Cards

Because of their limited features and various fees, prepaid cards are not good for daily use. You also will not be able to make any money from these cards, so use them only when it is absolutely necessary and not for everyday purposes.

The only time I use prepaid cards is when I get them as gifts.

CHAPTER FOURTEEN

The Best Hidden Credit Card Perk No One Uses: Free or Partial Free Travel

Reading and applying this one chapter from this book can open up endless travel opportunities you never thought would happen.

Is It Really Possible to Travel for Free?

If you keep an eye on the news on TV or anywhere else, you may have come across celebrity travel loyalists like Ben Schalapigg (Onemileatatime.boardingarea.com) or Brian Kelly (Thepointsguy.com) and many others who are travelling the world for free on rewards points mainly generated by credit cards or frequent flyer miles.

For example, Ben does not have a place to live because he is always flying first class and staying in upscale hotels around the globe. At 25, Ben already has flown five million miles on various rewards points, paying very little to none for his trip. Brian Kelly, the same as Ben, is also always flying and staying in hotels for almost free. While taking free travel to that extreme is unrealistic for most of us, it is still possible to score free or partially-free travel with a few credit card techniques and that's what I will talk about in the next chapter.

What to Expect

To be honest, it will be difficult to travel for free each year for everyone. However, you can easily score half of your travel free each year and/or one full travel (flight + hotel) every few years or so depending on how well you can use these techniques.

I use these techniques as well and each year I get to travel paying nothing or very little (either flight or hotel) and I also travel one trip 100% free every year on a business-class flight.

CHAPTER FIFTEEN

How to Travel for Free or Fly Business Class for Free or Paying Very Little

I will go over some basic stuff you need to know to travel free or partially free using your credit cards. All these techniques are legit and legal, so you are not breaking any law. Yes, applying them can be a hassle and time consuming, but that's what the drawbacks are to score free travel. I don't mind the pain, as I value and enjoy my free or partially-free travel.

You Have to Have a Good Credit Score

If you haven't been paying your credit card balances on time, have too much credit card balances (higher debt-to-credit or credit utilization ratio), have been applying for loans too frequently, and so on, your credit score will be lower and these techniques will not work. Credit scores range from 300 – 900 and the higher your score is, the more likely you are to succeed.

You Need to Understand How Rewards Points and Frequent Flyer Programs Work

Don't expect to travel for free or partially free without learning how rewards and frequent flyer programs work. Although I discussed a little bit about rewards points in this book, there is a lot more to learn.

I haven't talked about frequent flyer programs in this book, as this book is not about airline points.

Learning about various points and miles is not a hard thing to do and you do not need any previous knowledge. If you are starting from scratch, look at Ben's or Brian's websites I mentioned previously. The more you learn about how these programs work, the better you will be able to travel for free or partially free. If you do not want to learn frequent flier or hotel points programs, stick to proprietary rewards points (credit card companies' own points) and you still will be able to travel for free or partially free, but to a much lesser degree.

The Techniques

It's nothing complicated. The trick is that you need to keep applying for credit cards that offer bonus rewards points or miles. If you are in the USA, you are in luck because American credit cards offer the most generous sign-up bonuses I have ever seen. If you are in other countries such as Australia, Canada, Great Britain, etc., you still have opportunities to accumulate points from sign-up bonuses.

I am in Canada and I am travelling for free or partially free year after year.

Won't It Hurt My Credit Score If I Apply for Too Many Credit Cards?

As I mentioned before, to benefit from what credit cards can offer you, you need to be a responsible credit card user who has a higher credit score. My credit score is above 800 and when I apply for a few credit cards my score goes down slightly, but still stays above 800 and goes higher in six months.

So it won't hurt your credit score much if you already have a good one and it will bounce back in a few months.

Isn't It Bad to Have Too Many Credit Cards?

If you don't know how to manage your money, having too many credit cards can be bad. But for someone who is in control and wants to make money from credit cards, it's not bad to have too many credit cards.

I have more than 20 credit cards and my credit score is still high. Some of the travel loyalists who travel 12 months have 30 to 40 credit cards and still they have an 800 and above credit score. So there is nothing wrong with having too many credit cards when you know what you are doing.

How Many Credit Cards I Can Apply for Each Year?

In 2015, I applied for 10 credit cards to accumulate points. If you have an excellent credit score, applying for 1 or 2 credit cards every three months is perfectly fine. Just keep an eye on your credit score and adjust your application frequency based on changes to your credit score.

Also, once you are familiar with the process to travel for free or partially free, you will discover your own pace to apply for credit cards that you are comfortable with. A word of caution I would like to mention is that if you have a big loan or mortgage renewal or applications coming up, do not apply for any new credit cards that year and be safe the year before. Once you are done with your mortgage or big loan, you can resume applying.

Should I Keep or Cancel All These Cards Once I Get the Bonus Points?

If you have proprietary points, use them before cancelling any cards because you will lose them once you close that credit card account. If you have airline, hotel, or other points (which are not credit card companies' own points), you can cancel your cards once points have been deposited in those accounts because credit card companies can't access those accounts to take them out.

However, there are some cards you may not want to cancel even when paying the annual fee year after year because the benefits they provide surpass the annual fees. For example, I have credit cards that I never use and pay the annual fees because they provide free hotel nights, lounge access, companion flight for $100 each year, and so on. These benefits outweigh the annual fees.

What I Am Going to Do with All These Points and Miles If I Don't Know How to Use Them?

If you want to enjoy free or partially-free travel, there is no alternative to learning how these programs work. Free information on every frequent flyer or hotel program is available online. All you have to do is read and learn.

Learn each individual program you have accumulated points on, such as Aeroplan, Avios, Bonvoy, etc. If you don't know where to start, go to Boardingarea.com and start from there; this site has many other websites covering most of the popular programs.

If your sign-up bonuses give you credit card companies' own points (proprietary points), learn how to make the most of those points. Some credit cards (called Hybrid Cards) offer to convert their points to other hotel or flight points. You will always get more value from flight or hotel points instead of redeeming them for travel-related expenses directly with credit cards. So be careful with proprietary points and make the most of them by learning how to get most value out of them.

CHAPTER SIXTEEN

Bonus Credit Card Tips

Bonus Chapter

In this chapter, I will provide some credit card tips that you can possibly apply in any country or at any time. These tips are not in any order and some of them may have already been mentioned before, but I will have them again as this is a bonus chapter.

Keep in mind that some of these tips may not apply in your country 100 percent word-for-word. But by now you already have the knowledge to filter out what is and isn't relevant in your country.

Credit Reports Do Not Tell Everything

Although credit reports show lots of information, it may not things such as salary, unemployment benefits, social assistance, criminal records, medical records, pawnshop or payday loan transactions, prepaid credit cards, how much money you have in banks, your brokerage accounts, and so on.

Also, marriage does not merge your credit report with your spouse's report.

Annual Fees May Be Negotiable

Having a credit card with annual fees does not mean you always have to pay annual fees. Credit card companies may waive their annual fees if you can successfully persuade them to do so. On Ahmed Dawn Dot Com I have some articles on how to approach banks to waive their annual fees and you can go through them for further information.

However, keep in mind this is something that depends on factors such as your financial institutions, what kind of credit cards you have, what kind of consumer you are, how much you spend, and so on. I have had success in the past getting my own annual fees waived, but lately banks are moving further away from this practice. Regardless, it does not hurt to try.

Apply for The Same Credit Card More Than Once and Get More Rewards

If you love your card because it gives a lot of sign-up bonus, why not reapply for the same card every 2 or 3 years and get more points? This procedure is also good if you don't want to pay annual fees for the same card every year. Many rewards cards run 1st year no-fee promotions and this is an excellent way to take advantage of it.

The trick you need to master here is to figure out which cards are suitable for earning rewards bonuses again and again and which cards are not. Some credit cards apply restrictions on giving bonus points for the second time, meaning you can have the same card as many times as you want but you will get hefty rewards bonus only the first time. Research online to find these gem cards on which you can play application-recycle to get more points in your country. It's not something difficult to find online. All you need is the will and enthusiasm to make the most out of your credit cards.

One Late Payment – Many Punishments

Credit card companies punish late payment by charging a penalty such as a late payment fee, right? Wrong. One late payment can translate into several punishments such as late payment fees, an increased interest rate, possibly reporting to the credit bureaus, etc. The best thing to do is never be late on any credit card payments – ever. If you can't pay the full amount, at least pay the minimum amount due.

Credit Cards That Offer Lounge Access

You can access airport lounges without flying business class; there are credit cards that offer free lounge access passes. These credit cards offer various travel perks, among them lounge entrances. If you travel at least once a year, it makes sense to get one of these cards.

Credit Cards That Offer Free Companion Flight

Some credit cards offer free flight for one when you purchase one air ticket paid in full. These cards can save you a lot of money if the airlines associated with them can work for you. Search in your country if you have issuers offering free companion flight credit cards.

Never Pay for Travel Insurance

Travel insurance can cost a lot of money, but many credit cards offer travel insurance for free. Look for a credit card in your country that meets your needs. Keep in mind that you have to meet its criteria to be eligible for full coverage, so always read the fine print.

CHAPTER SEVENTEEN

How to Save Money on Travel or Vacation

This chapter is an additional chapter to help you with your travel. At one point, you will start travelling using the credit card perks and features I mentioned, so keep these tips handy for later. Always use the Internet to do your research and know a few techniques; you can save a lot of money on your travel or vacation.

Travel During the Slow Season

Airfare cost is the most expensive segment of your travel expenses and you can cut it significantly if you travel during your destination's slow season or off-pick time. Use the Internet to find out what is the off-pick for the places you are travelling to. Another advantage travelling during the slow season that I enjoy is that it's not too crowded and easier to move around and do some sightseeing.

Mind Which Days You Fly

By picking specific days of the week, you will also be able to save money on airfare. Flying volume is higher on Monday, Thursday, and Friday. If you avoid these days and fly other days, you will get better deals.

Book Early

Early booking always saves you money. If you book your ticket 3 months to 1 year ahead, your savings will be higher than if you booked just before the trip.

Packages Save You Money

Whether you are booking an all-inclusive vacation to Cuba or booking a flight and hotel to Las Vegas, booking trips together as a package will save you more money than booking them separately.

Use Reward Cards

99 percent of banks and credit card companies offer travel reward cards these days. Use one or several reward programs available in your country and earn reward points to travel for free or partially free.

Never Use a Hotel or Airline's Own Website

If you use airline or hotels' own websites, you will end up paying more than 3rd party websites, unless they are offering a sale. Try a few websites such as Expedia, Kayak, etc. first before you book your trip because prices can vary from site to site. There are sites that offer lowest price protection, so keep an eye out and if you find a better price you will get a refund for the difference.

Beware of Currency Exchange Rates

Know your destination country's currency rate before you leave. The airport or hotel's own currency shop usually will not give you the best possible rates. What I found out from various trips is that the small currency shops located outside in general offer the best rates. I only convert about $100 in my destination country's currency beforehand to keep it with me and I do the rest of the conversion at a currency shop in my destination country. Also, if you are using your credit cards you will get good currency rates because credit card companies get preferential currency rates due to their high volume of transactions every day. But make sure you are aware of what your credit card companies are charging you in currency conversion fees when you use your credit cards in foreign countries.

Research Always Pays Off

International travel is far different than domestic travel. You are going to a place where everything is different and likely nothing is familiar to you. Research well on the Internet about your destination before you step out into unknown territories. Use common sense and research all sorts of situations you will be dealing with. Here are some suggestions:

- How much would it cost to get from the airport to the hotel?
- Should I be taking a taxi or avoiding a taxi, as taxis in some countries are not safe?
- Are there any tricks the local stores will do to make me pay more?
- Should I avoid any specific locations?
- Is it safe to stay outside the hotel in the evening?

CHAPTER EIGHTEEN

Ahmed Dawn Dot Com & My YouTube Channel

Ahmed Dawn Dot Com (www.ahmeddawn.com) is a globally-popular website that I started just before publishing my first book Invest Now. This site has a vast wealth of financial, credit card rewards, points and miles, travel and other articles, including articles on saving money. I encourage you to visit this site any time.

If you are reading this book, there are some sections on Ahmed Dawn Dot Com you might want to check out, as there are articles focused on credit card and travel hacks.

My YouTube Channel www.youtube.com/adawn has nearly 700 video posts as of this writing. I cover a wide range of topics and you will find something that will be of interest for sure. Have a look and let me know your feedback in the comment section in any one of the videos.

Sample Postings from Ahmed Dawn Dot Com

Ten Wallet Tips You Need to Know Before Leaving Home

"Why carry something if you don't need it?" Twenty years ago, a senior taxi driver in New York City gave me that advice – the best wallet tip ever and I have been religiously following it ever since.

Today, I will share some wallet or purse tips you should follow to make your life easier, simpler, and safer.

1. Go through your wallet and get rid of everything you don't use on a regular basis. There is no point in carrying all the cards and receipts in your wallet. I keep only those I use every day. If I use a credit or debit card occasionally, I leave it home and only keep it with me when I will be using it.

2. At any point, you should know exactly what items are in your wallet. This way, if you lose anything you will be able to detect it right away, reducing your chances of being a victim if someone else gets a hold of your cards.

3. Make a list of everything you carry in your wallet. Write down your credit card number, customer service phone number, and anything else you would require to block your credit or debit cards in case of theft or loss of your wallet. Better yet, you can scan the back and front of all your cards as well. Keep this list handy at home, in your hotel safe, or online securely in such a way that you will have access to it when you need to call your financial institutions in case of emergency.

4. Do not carry your wallet in your back pocket. Thieves use very sharp tools to cut pockets and it's a lot easier to cut when it's in your back or rear pocket.

5. Be careful and pay attention to what's going on around you. Thieves work together in crowded places and try to distract you by pushing you, causing artificial arguments among themselves, or anything else to cause distractions so they can use that split second to grab your wallet while you are distracted.

6. Keep some cash separated from your wallet in a different place on you. If you lose your wallet, this ensures that at least you will have some money to get home.

7. Do not keep your home or car keys in your wallet. If thieves get a hold of keys, they will be easily able to access your home or car because it's not hard to find information (home address on driver's license, vehicle information on insurance or registration card, etc.), leading thieves to further carry on their operations.

8. Do not write your PIN number on the back of your cards or carry it with you in your wallet. Also, do not use your date of birth, postal code, or phone number as your PIN. If thieves have your wallet, they will have access to enough information to guess your PIN by going through your wallet.

9. Do not leave your wallet in a jacket, coat, or anywhere else if you're checking these items in a restaurant, movie theatre, or anywhere else.

10. If you are wondering what's in my wallet, here are the items I always carry with me if I am in Toronto:

    - One bank card (Interac card)
    - One credit card
    - Driver's license
    - Toronto Transit Commission Metropass

If I travel, I modify these items depending on where I am travelling to.

NB – You do not need to carry your rewards or points card anymore, as smartphone apps have the capability to carry these cards digitally on your smartphone.

6 Things You Can Do Right Now to Manage Your Credit Card Debt

Credit cards are a modern-day necessity and it's unrealistic trying to survive without them. However, if you are unable to manage them, credit cards can take over your life. Let's look at 6 simple things you can do right now to take charge of your credit card debt.

Stop Charging – If you have credit card debt that you can't pay in full every month, do not charge anything on the credit card unless you have the money to pay it. This is your first step towards managing your credit card debt.

Avoid Making Late Payments - Always pay on time and never make a late payment. Late payments can affect your credit score. Pay at least the minimum if you are unable to pay the full amount for any given month. I have seen people not pay a 70-cent bill thinking it would not make sense to pay this small amount. They ended up paying a penalty for late payment and affecting their credit score. A small amount can drag you down a lot if it's not taken care of in a timely manner.

Call and Ask – Call and ask your credit card companies for a lower interest rate and waive any penalty fees you may have incurred. Optimize balance transfer offers to lower your interest on credit card.

Pay Extra Amount – Pay whatever extra amount, whether it's a small or big amount, you can possibly arrange to pay towards your credit card balances every month. If you look at paying additional amounts in terms of a longer time frame, it will accelerate your debt-free endeavour a lot faster.

Be Aware of Credit Repair – The Consumer Reporting Act has rules regarding how long accurate information can appear in a report and no credit/fix companies have the authority to remove, erase, or change this in a consumers' file. Beware of these companies claiming to fix your file.

Take Charge of Your Finances - Learn about managing money, investing, and building wealth for your financial future. There are many independent personal finance websites like Ahmed Dawn Dot Com, Canadian government websites, and U. S. government websites to help you build your financial roadmap.

HOW A CREDIT CARD CALCULATES INTEREST

In Canada, a credit card company mainly uses two methods to calculate the interest you pay. The methods are the average daily balance method and the daily balance method. Although the methods are different, they generate the same interest charge. If you are interested in finding out which method your card uses, you can call their 800 number or you can find it in your credit card agreement brochure. Now let's look at these two methods.

Average Daily Balance Method - Your credit card has a billing period of 29 to 31 days. The average daily balance is just the average of your daily balance during your billing period. The average daily balance is calculated at the end of every month. Take the balance at the end of every day and add them up (A). Divide this total (A) by the number of days in your billing cycle to get average daily balance (B). B is multiplied by daily interest rate to get average daily interest amount (C). Now, to calculate the interest charge for the month, multiply C by the number of days in the billing period.

To get your daily interest rate, take your annual interest rate and divide it by 365. Also, your interest rate can be found on your monthly statement.

Daily Balance Method - This method is simpler than the average daily balance method. Instead of making one calculation at the month's end, the daily balance method calculates your interest at the end of every day of the billing period. The calculation method is simple. Take your daily balance and multiply that by the daily interest rate and add up the daily interest to obtain the interest for the month.

Purchases, Cash Advances and Balance Transfers - If you pay your balance in full, you never pay any interest. If you don't pay your balance in full, you're charged interest from the date you made these purchases until they're paid for in full. Some credit card issuers charge interest from the date the purchases are posted to your account. You're charged interest from the date you made the cash advance or balance transfer.

Let Your Credit Card Company Pay Your Interest - By paying your balance every month in full, you are actually using your card company's money for free for your full billing period. Your card company always wants you to carry a balance so they can charge you interest and that's how card companies make money.

If you are paying your balance in full, you are actually using your card company's money at their high interest rate for free. Let me give you an example. In September 2006, I bought five British Airways return tickets for my trip at approximately $2000 each. My total cost was $2000 x 5 = $10,000. Most of the card companies charge 20% annual interest rate. If I do an approximate calculation for $10,000 at 20%, my one-month interest charge would be $165. Yes, that's right. My one-month interest charge would have been $165.

But I avoided this charge by paying my balance in full and my card company definitely did not like it because they lost $165. If you look at this a little differently, you can say that I borrowed money for one month at 20% interest rate but I have not paid any interest because my credit card company paid it for me.

What do all these facts translate into? Know how you are being charged and what your interest rate is. Pay your balance in full. It's like using your card company's money at their expense.

CONCLUSION

A Wonderful Journey

It is hard to believe, but we are in the closing chapter of this book. I enjoyed every moment of writing it, and I hope you enjoyed every moment reading it. Since I published Invest Now, I have been contemplating publishing more books and have been working on it at a slow pace for the last few years. However, I decided to publish all my future books on the Amazon platform from now on. As a result, starting with Money Hacks all my books are available only on Amazon.

Where Do We Go from Here?

Using credit cards to their fullest extent is not a miracle. It is a combination of knowledge and discipline. Reading this book and forgetting about it after a couple of days will not do you any good unless you start taking action. I will consider my work successful if this book can make you determined enough to improve your life by taking positive action towards your future goals.

Aim for Little in The Beginning

Based on the techniques I mentioned in this book, it is possible to save a lot of money and travel for free or paying very little. However, it is unrealistic to assume that everyone will be able to use all of the techniques in their countries. If you follow only some techniques and it works out for you, I will consider my work a success.

Emotion and Risk

Credit cards and spending can be emotional matters and emotionally-driven decisions can be risky. Don't be an emotional shopper. Avoid unnecessary spending by not making emotional decisions; emotional decisions can be a recipe for disaster.

Feedback

Feedback is always welcome. Your opinions matter and I would like to hear them. Communication fosters a connection between readers and the author. Let me know if this book worked out for you—or even if it didn't. Let me know which parts of this book you find most helpful and which parts you think did not help and/or need more elaboration or clarification. Based on your feedback, I will update the future edition.

How to Contact Me

The easiest way to contact me would be to send me an e-mail. My e-mail address is adawn.net@gmail.com. Also, you can contact me by leaving a comment on my YouTube Channel: www.youtube.com/adawn; I will reply right below your comments.

The Journey Is the Destination

Readers like you inspired me to write this book. I thought I would share valuable knowledge and hopefully change someone else's life. I believe in what I said, and every word in this book came out spontaneously.

I enjoy writing for you and my journey across the world has taken me to my next trip: my next book. I have not decided yet what the name will be, but I am thinking about writing my travel experiences in Egypt.

I will start working on my next book shortly after this book is published. Don't forget to see my Egypt trip on my YouTube channel even before the book is published.

I hope to see you again and until then, remember: live for the journey, not for the destination. The journey *is* the destination.

CREDIT CARD HACKS:

What Credit Card Companies Don't Want You to Know
By Award-Winning Author Ahmed Dawn

The must-have guide for digital-age credit card users. Credit Card Hacks delivers surprisingly simple steps to use credit cards for savings and travelling the globe for free or paying very little.

Take your credit cards out of your wallet with confidence, knowing you can outsmart your card issuers to use all the perks and features they didn't want you to know. Award-winning financial author Ahmed Dawn reveals practical steps you can take to deep dive into the hidden benefits of credit cards through various walks of life. Jam-packed with timely information and timeless advice for global readers, Credit Card Hacks provides a realistic, doable plan to put you on the road to financial success and global travel by knowing the ins and outs of credit cards.

Every time you don't use a credit card properly, you lose an opportunity to earn a free point or mile. To help you get started with credit card benefits, this book will show you:

- How to Pick the Right Credit Cards
- How to Use Promotional Rate Offers
- What Credit Card Feature You Should Never Use
- The Hidden Credit Card Perk No One Uses
- How to Travel for Free/Fly Business Class Using Credit Cards
- And much more

Credit Card Hacks offers no-nonsense, precise, and to-the-point tools and motivation you need to start saving money travelling for you and your family.

www.ingramcontent.com/pod-product-compliance
Lightning Source LLC
Chambersburg PA
CBHW070452220526
45466CB00004B/I805